When Windows Turn Into Mirrors

On Aging in Only Middle Age

When Windows Turn Into Mirrors

On Aging in Only Middle Age

By

Robert L. Horn

ISBN: 1-58721-400-8

1stBooks - rev. 7/20/00

ABOUT THE BOOK

"When Windows Turn into Mirrors"
is an effort by the author to put his life
into perspective for himself.

But after many encouraging comments,
he decided to reach out to other "middle-agers"
who might be struggling with the idea of aging.
It's a troubling time for many.

I have spoken with many people
who truly feel old when they hit
the ripe, old age of 25
and also those
who refuse to be old at 85.

Regardless of where you fall
along that continuum,
life is to be lived.

In middle age,
as well as "old" age, I presume,
your future is equally as important
as your past.

"When Windows Turn into Mirrors"
is both a reflection on your life,
as well as a window to the future.

Reflect on each wisely
and with kindness,
for you will be rewarded
by both.

DEDICATION

To my children,
Christopher, Matthew & Jason,
who constantly remind me
that I'm aging;

To my mother,
who never lets it pass
that I am young;

To my wife, Brenda,
who strikes the balance between the two,
reminding me of who I really am
at this point in life.

INTRODUCTION

Aging is a natural part of life.
You're born, you live several years,
and you die.

Since most of us in this part of the world
spend many years traveling through life,
we often forget about the finish line,
for it is seems too distant.
Still, at some point it becomes more clear.
It hits you one day that there is far less in front of you
than there is in the rear.

Everyone is different, of course.
For some it is 40 years old,
some 50, others 60, some beyond,
but one day most everyone sits back and realizes
just how far they've come
and to where they're heading.

This book is an effort
on just one person's part
to reflect on the past,
but then to realize
that it's not yet over.

That there is much to be done
and plenty of time to do it.

So when your windows turn into mirrors,
make a decision to appreciate it all, but to also move on.
Move on, look forward, to what is the second part of your life,
not the end.

On Aging in Only Middle Age
- Some Reflections

TABLE OF CONTENTS

When Windows Turn into Mirrors
Life's Work
On Hormones & Hobbies
If Only Then
I Opt to Not
I Listen to Them Now
Just Not Fair
Wednesdays
Today
Not All Bad
Unlimited Potential
Apondering
What a Find
Just an Old Hippie
They Sneak Up on You
Time to Think
Re-inventing the Wheel
The Better You
A Trip South with My Son
Keep Grinnin'
They Don't Expect Much
I'm Glad I missed the Turn
Death Comes More Frequently Now
As I Thought I Was
Me Mum

WHEN WINDOWS TURN INTO MIRRORS

The future was bright
through that clear glass pane

I could see forever,
nothing to block my view

The whole world was out there,
but only for the door

Someone must have glazed over the glass though
and turned them into mirrors

For now the reflections
are greater than the view

For I see much more behind me
than I do in the fore

I used to have windows,
now I have mirrors.

LIFE'S WORK

Think for a moment what it would be like
if a life was graded
by how many people you've helped,
your life's work with others,
and not by the people with whom you've dwelt

If one's career was deemed successful
by the totality of your work
by the direction it took
and not the money you're worth

Imagine being judged
by your influence on the young,
by how, because of you.
Others treat others

I've never been rich
I've never owned a new car
or built a new house

Still, I think I've helped many people,
but I know I've helped some

I think some others are better
because of my life,
but I know my life was better
because of them

I think I've had a successful life,
but I know I've had a satisfying life

I never sought a lucrative career,
but then I guess I never tried.

ON HORMONES & HOBBIES

Never thought it would happen,
but you better prepare.
For when the urge is much less
than it was back there

When the scenery on the beach
is of the historical and avian form.
When nuzzling up to your significant other
is just to keep you warm.

For when you first notice their dog
during a walk in the park,
instead of a chance with its owner
there might be a spark.

So make plans now.
Get a hobby you really enjoy
for when you lose the urge.

The interest will always be,
but hobbies will be there to take over
when hormones take less time,
than the allure of amour.

Hobbies take up that time
you used to use to propagate
when thoughts of lust
begin to abate.

Hobbies bring you enjoyment.
You maybe build a thing or two,
just like hormones
in the past used to do.

Hormones and hobbies both have their place,
but the wisest engage in both.

For it happens
that the former gives way to the latter
and you gotta be ready
for what's then on your platter.

IF ONLY THEN

If I was then
what I am now,

Life would have been easier,
not such a hurry.
Things would slow down,
instead of so blurry.

If I was then
what I am now,

Sex would be making love,
parties a chance to share,
little kids a joy,
time to come up for air.

If I was then
what I am now,

The world would be smaller,
seeing all of us the same,
differences not so different
in this world-wide game.

Age gives you that perspective somehow.
If only I was then
what I am now

I OPT TO NOT

Young, eager and full of vigor

I like to see those things
that I used to do, but that now I don't.
I suppose I could, but probably won't.

The eagerness is still there,
but the energy is down,
so instead of a party,
just a ride to town.

Yeah, I'd love to run,
I love to play.
I'd like to give the decathlon a shot.

But at this late date
I opt to not.

I LISTEN TO THEM NOW

Probably the best lesson
I've learned over the years
is to listen to my elders.

They've been there,
they've done that.
They tried to tell you.
It wasn't just a chat.

They tried to tell you this.
they tried to tell you that.
It's not just space
under that old-fashioned hat.

Now you're a little bit older
and have much to give,
but the young aren't listening,
they have a life to live.

I listen to my elders now.

JUST NOT FAIR

The ability goes
the time runs short,
but the dreams are still there.
It's just not fair.

WEDNESDAY

I like Wednesdays
The worst of the work week is over
and the best is yet to come
It's Hump Day!

You've worked hard
The end is in sight
Still, it's only Wednesday
and there's still a lot to fight.

The week is a microcosm of life.
You're middle aged,
and you've done a lot,
but there's still more to do,
even those things you forgot.

Besides, it's only Wednesday.
I like Wednesdays

TODAY

Someone very wise once told me
that the best of everything will always be
that which was yesterday
and that which will be tomorrow,

For the past was good
and the future is bright,

So why can't ever
the future of yesterday
and the past of tomorrow be
today?

NOT ALL BAD

It's not all bad, though,
to have lived how you lived,
to have done what you've done.

It's actually kinda neat
to see what was there,
to look at your past.
So what if you have no hair.

It's not all bad
to be able to reflect,
to appreciate your life,
memories to collect.

It's not all bad
to have had what you had.

UNLIMITED POTENTIAL

I guess there are at least two ways
to look at "unlimited potential"
when you're at this stage in life.

Either your potential was completely realistic,
or it was over-stated,
over-believed by others or yourself,

Or it was unrealistic
for anyone in the first place,
given everyone's faults.

Initial expectations are hard to meet,
whether they're your own, your mom's or dad's,
or some teacher somewhere back in class.

So rationalizations have to occur,
soon or later, at this point in time.
You're where you're at now,
but is this where you were supposed to have been?
Given your unlimited potential,
given what you should be,
and given where you're at ?

Was unlimited potential
unrealistic all the while ?
Or was the potential really there
and you failed ?

The greatest gift in the world
is the ability to succeed,

But the pressure to achieve it
is the biggest burden indeed.

APONDERING

Sometimes you've seen
what others haven't seen,
been where others haven't been.

Sometimes you are
who others aren't.

Sometimes you've got a point of view
that, to them, is all so new.

Sometimes you can get 'em
to just ponder awhile,

Maybe walk down
that idea aisle.

Maybe not,
but just gettin' them apondering
is quite a bit.

Maybe your thoughts and their's
would be quite a fit.

WHAT A FIND

Ever sit in the sun
with your best friend ?

Wondering where they're at now,
inside,
and where they want to be ?

Knowing they're here
because they want
to be with you.

Knowing that you're here
because you want
to be here, too ?

You know them,
they know you,

But still, different people
and different dreams,
but still the same, it seems.

Ever sit in the sun
with your best friend,
appreciating it all ?

And then you realize
that after all these years,
that it's your spouse ?

What a find !

JUST AN OLD HIPPIE

Hippies were young,
free-spirited,
free-thinking,
and free-to-be-you.

It all sounded so good,
the free-love,
communes,
love-ins.

Hippies were always young,
with flowers
and beads
& make love, not war
& tie-dyed everything.

Not a care in the world,
except how things could be better
for all of us.

But hippies grow up.
They still want to be free,
but want others to help others.

They want all of us
to help the rest of us.

They want all of us
to be able to count on the rest of us.

It's a tough position,
wanting to be free
of others' demands,

But at the same time,
wanting a whole society
to be there for you
and you for them.

Unrealistic for now ?
I don't know, maybe,

But for some of us
the dream doesn't die,
it just fades a little.

I guess I'm just an old hippie
who doesn't push it much anymore.

THEY SNEAK UP ON YOU

Your Little kids
aren't little anymore.
They were babies
just last year,
with the diapers,
the wiping of a tear.

Now, they're men and women,
Moms and Dads,
with little ones,
their own lasses and lads.

I must've missed something,
when the time blew past,
but I know I didn't.
It just went so fast.

They must've been doing this all along,
this growing up stuff,
but since I wasn't watching,
enough is enough !

But we were pretty close,
them and I,
So I'm assuming
that sooner or later
they'll reveal the secret of their stealth,

Probably during the same conversation
when they want to know
how I got so old and lost my health.

TIME TO THINK

Age slows you down a bit,
gives you time to think.
Issues don't mean as much,
but then they mean even more.

Before, a decision had to be made.
It was of the moment.
Time of the essence.
It had to be now
or time would be spent.

But now it's better
to slow on down,
think a little longer,
to find solid ground.

The problem will be there.
It will still need to be solved,
but sooner or later
it will have evolved.

You're deeper now,
but not quite as quick,
to make a decision, that is,
but still make it stick.

Age slows you down a bit,
but it's good
that you take the time,
and have to have,
more time to think.

RE-INVENTING THE WHEEL

"Don't trust anybody over 30"
Remember that one ?

You knew you felt what you felt,
but you didn't feel
what now you know.

Thirty was old then,
now it's young.

Then you knew
that you knew it all.

Now you know more,
but also know
that you know nothing.

Yeah, we had a point.
Their ideas were old
and things should change.

But we never considered
the ordeal
of starting over,
of re-inventing the wheel.

THE BETTER YOU

You have a lot to learn
from the young.

They are a younger you,
your own young children
and their friends.

You tried to teach them
to be you,
but better.

You have a lot to learn from them,
for if you succeeded,
they are you,
plus many years better.

You have a lot to learn, you know,
from the better you.

A TRIP SOUTH WITH MY SON

Spring break is here.
He's soon to be a man.
Anything to do, son ?
No, I have no plans.

A trip south ?
Just you and me ?
We'll have fun,
you'll see.

Experiencing my son,
and him me,
but maybe less for him
than for me.

Just a short trip,
a week or so,
before he leaves
and before I go.

Talking, laughing,
living together alone,
the closeness
is a bittersweet moment.

Then back north,
the return,
a thousand miles
of saying good-bye.

I have no plan either, son,
but it's been a wonderful journey
from where you began
to where you've just begun.

A trip south ?
Let's do it, kid.
We'll have a blast !

But my sincerest wish ever
is that we run outta gas.

KEEP GRINNIN'

There are cycles in life.
There are ups
and there are downs.

It's all relative, of course,
but it's up to you,
for how can you have an up
with no down to compare it to ?

How can you feel down,
without having been up ?

Ups and downs are normal,
but until you've been through it,
several times,
none of it jibes.

It helps you through the bad,
for you know
that sooner or later
things will be better.

But then, too,
and you know the rest,
the ups that are now
will also never last.

There will be ups
and there will be downs.
There's losin',
then there's winnin'

So I figure the best way to look at it,
that cloud and silver lining thing,
is that regardless of the clouds,
soon you'll be winnin'

Be prepared then
and just keep grinnin'

THEY DON'T EXPECT MUCH

I'm not sure, but I don't think
they expect much of me now.

Looking for new ideas,
are all the young 'uns.
You're too old for the up'n comin's.

For you're on the wrong side of the future
for those who know the truth,
don't seem to expect much
anymore, of you.

But the elders,
the power brokers ?
To the keepers of the keys,
you're just a kid.

You'll grow into a fine leader,
but not yet long enough in our midst
to have paid your debt.
They don't expect much of you
yet.

It happens throughout life,
that too young,
too old thing,
but now it's really serious.

Neither one of them
expects too much of you
anymore or yet.

I'M GLAD I MISSED THE TURN

Before,
I was never satisfied with not having
what I knew I could get.

Now,
I've had a lot of things
that I never knew I wanted
and never knew I got.

I guess I should be disappointed
in not getting things
I must have wanted.

And I guess I should have tried
to get things I have.
But I'm not sure
which is which.

Did I not get the things
I tried to get ?
Or did I get the things
I didn't know I wanted?

It's too bad
that you can't know in advance,
so you could plan
to be ready to be where
you never thought you'd be.

And to be ready to be
the happiest you've ever been
without the things you didn't get.

Whichever,
I think I'm glad I didn't turn,
way back then.
I'm glad I missed the turn.

DEATH COMES MORE FREQUENTLY NOW

In your youth
you didn't see much death,
people close to you,
that is.

You didn't see it too often,
and when you did,
it was quite a shock.
Why them ?

Grandmas and Grandpas
sometimes go,
but it was usually
those who were old.

Your friends didn't die,
unless a terrible accident
or war.

These days it is closer,
not only your parents,
but also your friends.

I don't know why,
well, yeah, I do,
but it seems more realistic now
to accept that people die.

It's also more scary,
worse than it was
than when just a kid.

For when you were young,
I suppose you expected people to die,
those who were old,
but never lived nearby.

I know that passing on
is part of living,
is part of others moving on,
without you or without them.

But it seems that as you mature,
death comes more frequently
than it ever did before.

AS I THOUGHT I WAS

I hope you remember me,
not for who I was,
but for who I thought I would be.

I meant to be
a good parent
and I hope I was.

I tried to be
a good person
and I think I was.

I meant to be
a helper of others
and I know I was.

But the inward eye
is myopic
and not all too focused.

It seems to see what others may not,
For what you want others to see
may not be there at all.

The light you use
to see your own deeds
is not as bright in other people's eyes.

I hope you remember me
for who I thought I was,
for what I thought was me.

ME MUM

Sometimes you wonder
where you're from.

How'd I get here,
what have I become ?

Plenty of journeys,
but she's still there.

She does all the work,
it's just not fair.

She brought me out,
and at games she'd shout.

She watched my doubt
and brought me about.

Sometimes I wonder
where I'm from,

But I'd be nowhere
if it weren't for me Mum.

I love you, Mom
wherever I'm from.

On Aging in Only Middle Age
-Looking Forward

TABLE OF CONTENTS

Way Too Young to be Thinking That Old
Puppies in the Field
Plant a Sapling
The Shore
Life's Cycles
Happiness of Pursuit
Mind Like a Steel Trap
Life After Forty
Just Keep in Touch
Belly Laughs
Sunday Driver
Let 'em Talk
Lose the Antlers
Not Knowin' where You're Goin'
I Hope the Lights are White
Burning Bridges
Weeds
Enjoy what is Here
Separate From The Hurt
Indian Summers
Not Quite There
A Wednesday Decision

WAY TOO YOUNG TO BE THINKING THAT OLD

You're much too young
to be thinking
of only the past.

You're not old enough
to have even had
what others have already lost.

To reflect only on the past
is depriving you
of what could be,
if , of yourself,
you would only ask.

In what you feel is middle age,
it's easy to see
only what has been
and not what really can be.

So relish in your accomplishments,
appreciate your life
and what you have,

But it really is only Half-Time
and you've yet to play
the whole second half.

The rest is yet to be told,
for you're way too young
to be thinking that old.

PUPPIES IN THE FIELD

Puppies in the field
are a sign of life.

Ears flapping,
tails wagging.

Not a care in the world,
for they have you.

You give them
their every need.

And they give you even more,
their unconditional love.

You must be there then,
for them,

For they need you,
as do others in your life.

A full half-life may have already passed,
but there's much more to be done.

They must grow
and your support must not yield.

Besides, they kinda like ya' ,
those puppies in the field.

PLANT A SAPLING

Plant a sapling
when you first feel your age.

Care for it,
water it,

For it is the rest of your life
you've yet to see.

Spring will bring growth,
each and every year,
just as will yours.

Autumns will bring rest,
each and every year,
just as will yours.

Cherish it,
that new tree,
watch it grow,

For it is the rest of your life
you've yet to see.

There are always new beginnings
and paths to walk,
trees to climb
and times to turn the page.

Plant a sapling
when you first feel your age.

THE SHORE

The horizon is there,
ever expanding,
down at the shore.

Ever present,
always calling
for those at the fore.

It promises the future
with all it's hope,
with all it's allure.

Beyond that horizon
lies your future, too,
past that green
and under the blue.

The possibilities are endless,
but impossible to see.

It'll take a journey, though,
if you want it to be.

The beauty of the shore,
it's hopes,
it's dreams,
is hard to ignore.

LIFE'S CYCLES

Don't wanna walk
when you're young,
so ride bicycles.

Go to work
when you're grown,
so drive beat up cars.

Work for awhile,
drive better cars.

After years,
drive nice cars.

Environmentally sensitive,
take the bus.

No,
drive really nice cars.

Need some exercise,
ride bicycles.

Can't drive,
have to ride a bike.

Start out on a bike,
end up on a bike.

Maybe that's why they call 'em cycles.

The next one must be
just around the curve.

HAPPINESS OF PURSUIT

The happier times of my life
have always been
when I had a dream,
a goal to reach.

What you'll do,
all things accomplished
before you're through.

A meaningful relationship,
a successful life,
happiness,
a husband or wife.

Education, career
It didn't seem so serious,
but it wasn't just a game,
still there was always something
for which you had to aim.

The length of life?
The point was moot.
There would always be time
for another pursuit.

But what of the effort,
the time spent on the dream,
the journeys you took ?

Not the end,
but the means of that pursuit ?
And over the years
it's not the end,

but how you got there, it seems,
that makes up your memories,
your dreams.

So why change?
Choose something now
for which to shoot.

There's nothing better
than life, liberty
and the happiness of pursuit.

MIND LIKE A STEEL TRAP

Used to have a mind
like a steel trap.

You heard,
you remembered,
you understood.

The issues of the day
were readily at hand.
Whatever the problem,
you'd take a pretty decent stand.

There was logic,
analysis,
figures of speech,
and synthesis.

There was always
another point of view,
a chance to change
after thinking it through.

But that edge seems to abate,
a little at a time,
but still, if you try,
it's not too late,

If you realize what's going on,
that others' ideas
are still just as strong.

Close-mindedness is a slippery slope,
and actually degenerative,
when you have all the answers
and nothing to give.

Continue to always be aware
that more than you
have great things to share,

That others,
even the most different from you
have their own legitimate views
of how they see the news.

You used to have a mind
like a steel trap,
so don't get trapped
by a steel mind.

LIFE AFTER FORTY

Life just beginning after forty
maybe isn't always all that true.

But then you've never been there before,
so, to you, it is still all new.

Just as at the tender age of two
with so much to see,
so much to do.

In a sense then,
you are just beginning now,
searching from this perspective,
why to live and how.

But now you have so much more,
to build upon,
when you don't know
exactly what's in store.

Not all of us at this age
are able to retire,
maybe never will,
still, you more easily tire.

But it's a beginning,
a brand new start,
if only it can be found
in your more experienced heart.

Yeah, I guess life does begin anew
at forty, at fifty,
at sixty-two.

If only you don't give up,
and smile at the view
and do much more
than just seeing it through.

JUST KEEP IN TOUCH

Sometimes you think,
especially nowadays,
you know more than you do,
when more set in your ways.

It's easier to lecture
than to merely be here.

It's tempting to talk,
but not yet hear.

But in dealing with our young,
we have much to fear,
when we just keep speaking,
not stopping to hear.

Listen to them,
so they listen to you,
for you have much to offer
with you being you.

The next part of your life
could mean so much,
to you and to them,
if you use the time
to just keep in touch.

BELLY LAUGHS

Laughter is good for the soul.
It keeps ya' young
when stress takes it's toll.

When you're a child,
laughs come easily,
but steadily become more mild.

We can float through the whole week
without ever showing
a crease in the cheek.

Even a chuckle, a grin
is better than nothing,
but better yet
is just ole belly laughing.

Makes your face contort,
makes you hurt,
maybe even
makes you snort.

Who cares what they say,
a belly laugh
each and every day.

That surely will
keep the doctor away.

SUNDAY DRIVER

You know 'em,
the ones you're behind
when you're trying to be on time.

Havin' their leisure,
enjoying the view,
slowing down
to annoy only you.

To take in the scene,
I, too, now tend
to move a little slower
around the bend.

I see things more clearly
when I slow to observe
what is here and may be
around the curve.

There are lakes, woods,
a meadow, a stream.
They're all there
with a little less steam.

I'm a Sunday Driver these days,
seeing what's there
and slowing my ways.

Try being a Sunday Driver,
if you get my gist.
You don't even want to know
what you've already missed.

LET 'EM TALK

You'll be surprised
at what you're remembered for,
the good, the bad,
but your kids know the score.

Let them talk
about their childhood,
not what you remember,
but what they understood.

It's really their impressions
of what they recall,
not your's,
that's more important, after all.

For that's how you raised them
and you need to know
how to explain it
or how to amend the show.

But let 'em talk,
your kids,
about their childhood,
sometimes scary,
but mostly good.

Actually listen
to how they grew,
through their own thoughts,
and not those of you.

The things you may remember
didn't happen at all
as far as they
can easily recall.

LOSE THE ANTLERS

You've fought your share,
but you should now discover
that battles were won,
but the rut is over.

You certainly still have
ideas to be sold,
plenty to say,
and lots to be told.

Still, the weight of the horns,
the weapons of old,
might come in handy,
but can get in the road.

These days, lose the antlers
and lighten the load.

NOT KNOWIN' WHERE YOU'RE GOIN'

What do ya' do
when you've not a clue
of what to do?

You find yourself here
at the end of the pier
with no boat to steer.

You did your best.
You passed the test,
so on now to your next
unknown quest.

So here comes another boat,
maybe something else
to keep you afloat
and your life to devote

So make a cry
Give it a try,
so it'll not again
float on by.

It's quite okay,
in this life's bay,
just not knowin'
exactly where you're goin'.

I HOPE THE LIGHTS ARE WHITE

Oft' as I feel "Old Dolly" swerve,
as o'er the rails we fare,
I look up at the starry dome
and wonder "What is there?".

For who can speak for those who dwell
beyond the starry sky,
for no man yet has lived to tell
just what it means to die.

The Blue light marks the crippled car,
the Yellow signals "Slow",
the Red light is the "Danger" light,
the White light, "Let her go".

Ft. Wayne was our terminal,
where we would come to rest.
Of all the places on the road,
the one we loved the best.

Swift towards life's terminal I trend,
the run seems short tonight.
God only knows what's at the end.
I hope the lights are white.

Gale Beerbower
For Glenn A. Phillips
Locomotive Engineer

BURNING BRIDGES

Over the years,
throughout your life,
some relationships end,
at times, due to strife.

It happens to everyone,
whether you like it or not.
You may try to save it,
but often cannot.

You're over the gap then,
when you cross that bridge,
but the gorge remains
between ridge and ridge.

It may not seem likely now,
in the heat of the break,
but you never know
what later may be at stake.

You may someday want to return
and regain that place
when you or they wish
a return to grace.

But if that bridge has already been burned
through a horrible word
or devastating deed,
reconciliation will go unheard.

Bridges ought to be fire-retardant,
unable to burn,
to be re-crossed
to what might later be yearned.

Bridges go in both directions,
cross it, but able to return,
rethinking the loss,
and maybe return.

WEEDS

A weed is a plant
that you didn't plant.

My brother once asked,
why do I pick dandelions,
the color of yellow,

So that now I'll have room
to plant flowers
the color of yellow?

Things come along
throughout your life
that at first
you truly dislike,

Then you may wonder why
the things you want
are so much alike
the things you don't.

So, before you pull,
think about the weeds,
those which may later
just meet your needs.

ENJOY WHAT IS HERE

I've told myself many times
over the years
to enjoy what's here.

To hope for more
is to invite heartache
and many a tear.

The absence of today's gladness
is the making of the next day's sorrow.
Through no one's fault
what is here today
may not be tomorrow.

But it's not healthy
to wish the good times never existed
in order to ease the fall,
for the spirit was light
and to deny that
would be to not have existed at all.

SEPARATE FROM THE HURT

Are you in a place
where your children
and you
are in a different space?

Reflecting back,
so many years ago,
where you brought them up
and helped them grow?

Now away on their own,
they're gone
and forget you're here
somehow.

The hurt's so bad
it's hard to take,
but nothing to be said,
for the children's sake.

Then, for some small wish
you ask and you pray,
but they turn you down.
They still refuse to play.

The anger turns to hurt,
but you don't know what to say.
You think of death,
so you're not in the way.

Maybe it's time now
to think of you,
time to look forward,
to begin anew.

For they're over there
and you're right here.
There can be no more heartbreak
for you to fear.

Your attention from them
you decide to divert,
to separate yourself
from all the hurt.

INDIAN SUMMERS

There is spring, later there is fall.
In everyone's life, times to rejoice, times to recall.

Between the two is the summer breeze,
the warmth, the joy, a time of ease.

Sometimes, though, autumn
comes way too soon
with not enough time
to see it through.

Spring and summer
are hard to leave,
but in the good that's there,
you have to believe.

What was produced in spring
was cared for, nurtured, given life,
so there is much still there.
You may be a daughter, sister, mother and wife.

What has been nurtured
through the joys of summer,
the times of you,
will be strong enough
to begin anew.

Because of your efforts,
they'll continue to live,
to remember, to love
all you had to give.

Often though
with the blow of the early winds,
the sun appears
and Indian Summer begins.

A remission of sorts,
a gentle reprieve
just when all others
were beginning to grieve.

With Indian Summers
you have the fruits of spring,
the joys of summer,
the time to again begin.

Year after year,
if only in my mind,
they seem to appear.
Believe in Indian Summers.

NOT QUITE THERE

At this point in my life
there's somewhere
I gotta' be,
but I'm not sure where.

There's something to be done,
someone to be,
somewhere to go,
something to see.

There's a feeling
that it's not too far,
that it's less distant
and maybe even near.

I couldn't know,
but it's fairly clear,
that it's not all bad
to just be here.

But there's a point at which
I gotta be,
but I'm not sure where.

All I know
is I'm not quite there.

A WEDNESDAY DECISION

The middle of the week
in the middle of life.
Is it time now
to take another direction ?
Do something different ?

That thing you always wanted to do
or that crazy notion you had
when you were but twenty-two.

Yeah, dreams appear,
but priorities change.
It really is okay
to think not only of yesterday,
but also of today.

Besides,
It's only Wednesday in your life.

You could stay where you are
and try it on the side.

A new dream,
a new idea.

Something you never tried
on the other side of life.

Or you could just drop out
and go ahead full steam.
But you can't let go by,
what is now your dream.

Make a Wednesday decision
or at least a decision to try.

ABOUT THE AUTHOR

Bob Horn is an active 50-something father of three sons, Chris, Matt & Jason.

As a Navy veteran, special education teacher, wrestling coach, baseball coach, tennis coach, Scout leader, attorney, carpenter, woodworker, family mediator, paralegal & writer (some formerly and some currently), he is living proof that times and people change and that there is always a past, as well as a future. Both need to be explored.

The author was born and raised in Fort Wayne, Indiana, and currently resides in Bradenton, Florida, with his wife Brenda, a Physical Therapist and published photographer.

Together, they attempt to focus on not only what they have, but also what was, what wasn't, and that which might or will be tomorrow.

After all, if you take away the possibility of an Olympic Gold Medal, most things are still possible in <u>only</u> middle age.

Life may or may not begin at 40, but Bob Horn is as happy now as he's been in his entire life, save for the loss of hair and the gain of gut.

www.ingramcontent.com/pod-product-compliance
Ingram Content Group UK Ltd.
Pitfield, Milton Keynes, MK11 3LW, UK
UKHW040017200726
13854UKWH00001B/243